Dear Diary

The Art and Craft of
Writing a Creative Journal

Joan R. Neubauer

Library of Congress Cataloging-in-Publication Data

Neubauer, Joan R.
    Dear diary: the art and craft of writing a creative journal/Joan R.
Neubauer.
        p.   cm.
    Includes bibliographical references
    ISBN 0-916489-61-2
    1. Diaries-Authorship.   I. Title.
PN4390.N48   1995
808'.06692-dc20   95-49501
                                                        CIP

Copyright © 2002
MyFamily.com, Inc.

Published by Ancestry® Publishing,
an imprint of MyFamily.com, Inc.

P.O. Box 990
Orem UT 84059
www.myfamily.com

First printing 1995
10   9   8   7   6   5   4   3

Printed in the United States of America

This book is dedicated to the loving memory of my grandmothers: Rose Aquilone, whose journals are lost to me forever, and Isabella Belmont, who taught me how to remember.

CONTENTS

ACKNOWLEDGMENTS

First, I would like to acknowledge my husband, Steve—my life's partner, best friend, and critical editor—for his endless encouragement and understanding of the many hours I spend writing. Thanks also to my children—Regina, Julie, and Stephen—for their help at home and for how proud they sound when they tell their friends their mom is a writer.

I have also been blessed with many friends, most of them writers, who have rejoiced with me when I succeeded and shared my grief at rejection. Thank you, Barbara Reeves, Toby Singhania, and Joan L. A. Reeves. You help me keep my perspective and sort things out.

With gratitude, I remember the booksellers and program chairmen who have invited me to talk with people, lead workshops, and sign books. I would also like to acknowledge the many people who attended my workshops and gave me the idea for this book.

Finally, I would like to say a very special thank you to Loretto Dennis Szucs, the kind of editor every writer prays for.

PREFACE

I consider myself fortunate in many ways, including the fact that I knew all four of my grandparents. All were strong individuals. Three of the four left family and home to travel across the Atlantic to seek a new beginning. The hardships of weeks at sea were nothing compared to the goal of a brighter future they held in their hearts. They married, worked hard, and raised large, caring families. Now they are gone and all I have are memories: the scent of Prince Albert tobacco commingling with the aroma of long simmering spaghetti sauce, a boisterous laugh and books filling the house.

My mother's mother, Isabella, came to this country alone when she was only sixteen. I regret that I never asked her how such a young girl managed to pay the price of her passage in steerage. It would have told me so much about her. What I do know is that while Isabella never learned to read or write, she always remembered where she came from. As I grew up in her house, not more than two blocks away from more aunts, uncles, and cousins than my young mind could count, she taught me to take pride in my Italian heritage, but at the same time reminded me to thank God for having been born in America.

In contrast, my father's mother, a child of Italian immigrants, was born in New York City. Rose attended school, where she learned the joys of poetry and studied music and history. She was a voracious reader, and her house was filled with wonderful books and their heady smells of paper, ink, and glue. It was such a comforting balm that on my first visit to a public library I felt happy and content. And why not? It reminded me of grandma's house.

Several years ago my Uncle Lou told me that Grandmother Rose had kept a running journal during most of her life, relating her life's experiences in various ways. She filled her notebooks with poetry, stories, and thoughts from her heart. When I asked my uncle what had happened to her notebooks, he simply shook his head and said they were gone.

I wish I could go back through time and ask Isabella the questions I should have asked when she was still with me. I wish I could tell Rose I'd love to have her journals for safekeeping. I would tell my grandmothers that I want to know more about them, that I want my children to know the marvelous women they were. And though I can't turn back the tides of time to retrieve answers or notebooks, I can look to the future. I can keep my own journal and encourage others to do the same.

Perhaps my lack of knowledge about my own grandparents is the reason journals and autobiographies have become so important to me. Perhaps my own foray into genealogical research has left me wishing that those who came before me had left something more personal than a sheaf of official documents for me to peruse.

Whatever my reasons, whatever yours, I commend your decision to keep a complete and creative journal and to make it the best, the richest writing you've ever done. After all, your journal can become part of your legacy to those who come after you—a bridge to the future.

Part 1

History &
Philosophy of
Journal Writing

CHAPTER I: HISTORY

*T*he history of journal writing goes back many centuries to some of the world's oldest civilizations. In ancient Greece, astronomers developed the "ephides," a daily log in which they chronicled the positions of heavenly objects. In tenth-century Japan, ladies of the court kept "pillow books" in which they recorded their dreams and secret hopes.

During the Middle Ages, people began to keep journals and autobiographies as they became aware of their value as individuals. *Confessions,* by St. Augustine, and *History of My Calamities,* by Peter Abelard, of *Heloise and Abelard* fame, are two of the most famous accounts of this period.

British royalty also began recording the events of their reigns. But the rich and famous were not alone in their quest to be remembered. Many educated members of the newly emergent middle class felt a desire to leave a written legacy, and a few of their journals and autobiographies still exist, such as that left behind by Margery Kempe, a fifteenth-century, middle-class Englishwoman, whose diary is a written record of her religious beliefs and trials and tribulations with Church officials.

Most journals, in these early days, were kept by women. We in the twentieth century can only guess why. Perhaps this was due to the fact that a personal journal was one of few places women could enjoy complete freedom of expression, or perhaps women quickly realized the many benefits to be derived from keeping a journal and shared their thoughts with their friends. Whatever the reasons, the popularity among women of keeping a diary continued to grow.

Victorians of nineteenth-century England raised journal writing to a high art. Again, because of the many strictures society placed upon half its population, women found a friend, confidante, and therapist between the pages of a secret diary. At the same time, increasing numbers of men also began to put pen to paper and record their thoughts.

In the early days of the twentieth century, the popularity of journal keeping waned. Life moved faster, time shrank, and fewer people took the time or made the effort to keep a diary. Teenage girls were the exception. Possessing a book held closed with a lock made it safe to confess every feeling and thought to the pages inside. And even though these girls eventually grew up and lost interest in keeping a diary, generations of girls who came after them carried on the tradition.

People from a variety of professions such as psychologists, runners, clerics, and medical doctors are once again recognizing the many benefits to be obtained from keeping a journal. And it may be that aging baby boomers, wishing to send a message into the future are largely responsible for a renewed interest in journals.

Weight loss programs instruct participants to keep a food log to help them understand and change destructive eating patterns. Therapists instruct patients to keep a diary to work through grief and anger, and to express the more positive emotions of love and hope. Runners keep a log to track their progress. Some in the medical profession have found that keeping a journal can boost the body's immune system and help patients deal with chronic pain.

With so much interest, with so many reasons, I urge you to learn from the past, apply it to the present, and leave a legacy for the future. Start writing your journal today.

CHAPTER 2: PHILOSOPHY

*P*erception is reality." I'm sure you've heard or read this aphorism sometime, somewhere. On the surface, it simplifies even the most complicated situation: thinking something to be true makes it so. However, we know that simply believing that 2+2=5 doesn't make it reality. There's more to it than that. What those three words really mean is that our beliefs have a profound influence on the way we think and the way we perceive the world around us—in short, the way we operate.

Take a moment to think about yourself. If you're like many people, you feel that your life is mundane and of no special interest to anyone. You get up in the morning, march through your daily routines, and go to bed. Granted, ninety-nine percent of us do not live the lives that are the stuff of bestsellers, but upon closer examination, our lives are far from boring.

Each day we negotiate a tangle of schedules generated by work, children, family activities, and other responsibilities we must meet every day: car pools, doctor appointments, sports, classes, shopping, banking, meetings, and paying bills, to name just a few. Such a plethora of activity is enough to drive anyone to distraction, but it is definitely not boring.

Keeping a journal may just afford you the opportunity to look at your life a bit more objectively and gain a new perspective. When you look at yourself as, say, a character in a book, you begin to realize that what you have to say has merit, that what you do is important. With such a belief as your guide, you can create the opportunity to operate with a more positive attitude, and in turn, live a more enriched life.

On one level this book is about journal writing, but there is more to writing in your diary than just recording daily activities. Journals serve three very specific purposes.

PROVIDE A LEGACY

The first purpose of keeping a journal is to provide a legacy for those who come after us, much like a bridge between the present and the future. What we write about connects what we have learned and how we learned it. We can help those who follow us to understand the importance of our values and morals by demonstrating how we lived our life. I can think of few tributes greater or more touching than if my great-grandchildren read my journal a hundred years from now and with a knowing nod say, "Yes, she was right."

OUR AUTOBIOGRAPHY

The second purpose of a journal, one that is becoming increasingly recognized, is for the journal to eventually serve as the foundation for an autobiography. Most of us are too busy to sit down when we are twenty, thirty, or even forty years old, and write our complete story. We're busy raising families and building careers. But we can all find the few minutes a day it takes to write about the day's events. Later, when we decide it is time to put our life story into a book, half the work is already done. All we need do is compile entries from our journal and edit them into a single volume. In fact, this is the idea behind my earlier book, *From Memories to Manuscript: The Five-Step Method of Writing Your Life Story* (Salt Lake City: Ancestry, 1994).

From Memories to Manuscript breaks down the otherwise overwhelming task of writing your autobiography into five easy steps that anyone can follow: research, organize, write, edit, and publish. If you keep a journal, you are performing the first three steps on a day-to-day basis, a fact that will make completing the final two steps much easier.

OPEN UP NEW AND EXCITING PERSPECTIVES

Finally, a journal, especially a detailed, creative journal, serves a third purpose by helping us to attain a new and positive perspective on our life. Writing every day is a wonderful way to sort out the day's events and deal with the ramifications and resulting emotions. Putting our experiences on paper allows us to look at ourselves more objectively. We can better determine our strengths and weaknesses, and as a result, better recognize ways we can grow and improve. But we cannot achieve such growth if we travel from day to day without some reflection and evaluation of our life's events. A good journal is the vehicle by which we can help ourselves accomplish such personal evolution.

In the course of this book you will read about journal writing in relation to two broad categories: mechanics and abstracts. Mechanics deals with the *who, what, when,* and *where* of journal writing, which is all very basic, but important when you keep a journal. Among the abstracts, you'll learn some fiction techniques regarding plot and characterization to help make your writing exciting. You'll learn how to use them as if you were writing a novel.

I invite you now to turn the pages, to read and learn how to write a rich and exciting journal, and, in turn, begin to live your life with a new and richer perspective.

Part 2
The Steps

CHAPTER 3: MECHANICS

The concept of journal writing brings to mind several items under the broad umbrella of mechanics, including such details as who should keep a journal, what to use as your journal, what to write with, where to write, when to write. Perhaps the list seems too elemental to think about, but I assure you, these considerations are important in developing the discipline you need to write in your journal on a regular basis.

WHO SHOULD KEEP A JOURNAL?

Over the years I have met hundreds of people of many cultures from around the world, in all professions and trades, with varied levels of education and diverse political persuasions. As I spoke with them and got to know them, they eventually began to tell me about themselves. Not one has been boring. Everyone has a story worth telling.

Some people have related stories of flight from an unbearable political situation or religious persecution. Others have told of escaping an abusive childhood or living as a mercenary in a Third World country. Others simply told me of another way of life in far-off countries, about their families, friends, and jobs.

Don't think you must brave unusual dangers or live a hundred years before you have something worth saying. Everyone has a story to tell, even young children. Let me tell you about a six-year-old boy I know.

Adam (not his real name) is a happy child from a close-knit family. He attended the same elementary school as my son, and he waited with us at the bus stop. Every morning he emerged from his house with a smile on his face bright enough to rival the sun, even on Mondays. On one particular Monday morning Adam was especially cheerful and I asked him why.

With a great deal of enthusiasm he proceeded to tell me all about his weekend. "We went to San Antone and I saw my granddad. He did magic tricks and pulled quarters out of my ears, and he told me stories about when he was a cowboy. He even showed me his cowboy gloves! Do you know you could still see where the campfire burned his glove? And where a rope tore up part of the leather."

Obviously Adam had a great relationship with his granddad and loved him dearly. Then one Monday morning as he came to the bus stop, I noticed he wasn't his usual sunny self. Instead of running, he shuffled. He looked down at the ground rather than straight ahead ready to meet the world head-on. Instead of a smile, he frowned. Curious about his atypical behavior, I asked him what was wrong.

"We went to San Antone this weekend," he said then looked down at his shoes and sniffed.

His reply confused me because I knew how much he loved going to San Antonio.

I said, "I thought you liked to go to San Antone to see your granddad." He looked back down and murmured, "I did, but I had to say good-bye to my granddad this weekend."

"Why? Did he move?" I was hoping for a simple reason for Adam's sadness, but in my heart I knew something much more serious had happened.

Adam shook his head and whispered, "No, my granddad died this weekend."

My heart sank for that little boy and I wanted to hug him and tell him everything would be all right. To my surprise he looked up into my face, his eyes brightening as he reached into his backpack and pulled out a pair of worn, torn leather work gloves.

He held them out to me and said, "Because I was the oldest grandson, my grand-dad gave me his cowboy gloves. Look here," he said pointing. "This is where they got burned in the campfire and here's where the rope tore them up."

His expression softened as he said, "I'll miss my granddad. He won't be telling me any more of his cowboy stories and he won't be pulling any more quarters out of my ears. But as long as I remember his stories and have his gloves, I'll always have my granddad."

Such wisdom from a six-year-old child! But I think it's something we all knew at one time and along the way forgot. Sometimes we need a little nudge to remember.

In the same way that Adam treasures his grandfather's stories and cowboy gloves, someone may cherish our words some day in the distant future. Think of your jour-nal as a beautiful bridge between generations, a way to travel into the future and begin a relationship with others long after we have said good-bye.

Ideally, we should begin this journey as children to establish and nurture the habit of writing every day. Maybe in the beginning the pages will read like a litany of skinned knees and bruised egos, but all those things have a part in making us the adults we become. That's why it's important for us to encourage our children to keep a daily record filled with events and musings.

If you're past childhood, it's not too late to start. Today is, after all, the first day of the rest of your life. The you who will exist tomorrow deserves the opportuni-ty to look back and remember yesterday with clarity.

WHAT SHOULD I USE FOR A JOURNAL?

You have several options available, and you can have some fun experimenting until you find which you like best. For traditionalists, a journal just isn't a journal unless it's a book you can hold in your hand. They love the smell of the glue and paper, the sound of turning pages. For these people who admire the golden age of journal writing, I'd advise you to visit your local stationery stores.

There are beautifully bound books boasting a variety of colored papers, both lined and unlined. If you prefer a bit more privacy, there are diaries that come complete with lock and key.

Another option is a three-ring binder. These binders come in all sizes and can be filled with lined or unlined paper. Perhaps you'd prefer a simple composition notebook bound like a book. The important thing is to find something you are comfortable handling. Whatever your choice, you must come to love this journal as much as you cherish a favorite novel or other book you simply cannot part with. You must be so happy with your choice that you look forward to writing in it regularly.

Do you remember how you felt when you were a child in the weeks just before school started? I looked forward to picking out school supplies. I went to the store with my mother and bought new notebooks, pencils, and crayons. With a kind of anxious glee, I picked out new rulers and pens and packs of paper. It was a great feeling.

When I got home with my booty, I placed the paper in my new binder and carefully arranged the dividers. Once I had organized everything, I could hardly wait until the first day of school so I could finally write on those crisp new pages with my newly sharpened pencils. You should feel the same way about the book you choose for your journal.

Since you want this book to last for many generations, you should use acid-free paper, which will not yellow, crack, or degenerate over time. Most stationers and some office supply stores carry such paper.

WHAT SHOULD I WRITE WITH?

Your book is not the only item to consider if you are going to hand write your journal. You must also give some thought to your writing implement. Some people say they like to use a refillable pen that is different from the pens they use to compose their shopping list or pay bills. They're willing to spend extra money for a good, refillable pen. They confess to splurging for their journal writing pen, spending far more than they'd spend on an ordinary pen but, then, this particular pen is for something very important: it is to be kept with the journal and used exclusively for journal writing. How much you spend depends on you. Whatever you decide, view your pen as something special.

The idea of exclusivity plays an important role in forming the habit of writing in your journal on a regular basis. If you consistently write with the same pen in the same book, you will condition your brain to get you in the mood to write. In such a frame of mind, the words will flow more freely. You may even surprise yourself when you discover a latent talent for writing.

On the other hand, you may choose to take advantage of modern technology for your journal. I highly recommend using a computer or word processor for speed and flexibility. I love my computer and would be lost without it, since I use it for a multitude of tasks, including journal writing. I still maintain exclusivity because I keep my journal computer files in a separate directory or on a special disk.

If you opt to use a computer, you can keep it simple by using a word processing program with which you are already familiar. However, software is available which sets up pages for each entry complete with date and time. Many programs offer a search function that allows you to find specific dates, names, or phrases.

Sophisticated, user-friendly programs also allow you to write, move blocks of text, and check your spelling! Spell check is a feature I bless every time I sit at the computer since my brain sometimes gets ahead of my fingers. This micro technology is a wonder that permits you to edit as you compose and in a short time write error-free journal entries, which you'll want to print and file away for safe keeping.

Whichever you decide upon, choose a program that you are comfortable with. You don't want technology to get in the way of your creativity.

You will, of course, eventually want to bind your pages in some way, and you have many options, from a three-ring binder to plastic spiral binding, to a gold-embossed, leather-bound book. (There are binderies that will bind a single volume in this way.) The price range for these options varies from a few dollars to as much as a hundred. I advise you to buy the best you can afford. Remember, this book is intended to last for a very long time.

Whether you choose a manuscript book and elegant pen, or a keyboard and a computer for your journal is unimportant. The important thing is that you keep one. Don't feel intimidated if you use pen and paper, whether by choice or necessity, as opposed to using more sophisticated technology. If you use a computer, don't feel you're missing the magic of holding a bound book in your hand; you can easily bind your printed pages later.

Remember, you're not competing with anyone over how sophisticated your writing tools are, or how heavy a journal you can create. You are recording your experiences for yourself, right now; and for others in the future.

WHERE SHOULD I WRITE MY JOURNAL?

The place you choose as your writing spot is as important as anything else we've discussed. Focusing on the goal of writing regularly, you should choose a single place in which to write every day. We are creatures of habit and gain comfort from doing the same things in the same places. Writing is no different. Professional writers often say that writing in a familiar place helps them to accomplish three important things regarding their craft.

First, writing in the same place helps in a very practical way to stay focused since there's nothing new to look at in the "old writing corner." The same pictures and wallpaper have been hanging on the same walls for years. In a familiar environment, you know where everything is, so that when the phone rings, you can reach for it without looking up or losing your train of thought. Eventually, you'll fit into your space as easily as you fit into a pair of comfortable, old slippers.

The second reason to establish a particular place for your writing is that familiarity brings a certain comfort level with it. If you are comfortable, you'll be able to tap into your creativity more easily and overcome distractions and obstacles.

The third, and perhaps most important reason of all to establish your own writing place, is that the sameness of place, together with the sameness of time, serves to reinforce the habit of writing. Just as we have been conditioned to eat in the kitchen and sleep in the bedroom, we can condition ourselves to write in a particular place.

Don't undertake other tasks in your journal corner, such as paying bills. Devote this space exclusively to journal writing. That will help your brain do the bidding of your heart more consistently, making it easier to successfully write a journal.

While the causes are many, discomfort and unfamiliarity top the list for one of the most dreaded obstacles among writers: writer's block. Writer's block is an insidious malady that creeps into your brain, and, like a little voice, urges you away from your writing goals. But take heart, it can be cured. Let me suggest a technique that might work for you.

Walk away from your journal, take some deep breaths; perhaps get a glass of water. Try doing something completely different for fifteen or twenty minutes: fix a snack, tinker with a gadget you need to fix, or make a to-do list for the next day. In any case, think about something completely different than what you're trying to write about. In a few minutes, you should be ready to sit down and get back to your writing.

But this is not the only cure for writer's block. If you ask a hundred writers about how they deal with the problem, you'll get five hundred solutions. You may even come up with a few ideas of your own. The important thing is to realize that writer's block happens and you can deal with it. It can also be eased by maintaining focus, comfort and familiarity.

WHEN SHOULD I WRITE IN MY JOURNAL?

I have a writer friend who takes a few minutes each morning, before beginning work on her current project, to write about her previous day. She tells me it's her special time to put the day's events into perspective. She saves the completed entry, prints it, and "hides it" in a folder. Then she faces the new day with a fresh outlook.

I encourage you to write in your journal at the same time every day. For some people, the most productive time is late at night, just before bed, while memories of the day are still fresh. These individuals say they can picture things more vividly, and in turn carry that clarity into their writing.

Others find that the first thing in the morning, when their mind is fresh, works best. They like to take a quiet moment and review the previous day. They feel they can look at yesterday more objectively and with a more alert mind. You should find the time that's best for you.

While a daily regimen is the most desirable, don't throw away your newly purchased diary because the daily commitment feels too burdensome. If once a week suits your busy schedule better, then set aside a certain time, perhaps every Sunday afternoon, to recall the week's events, and record a things that stand out in your mind. Writing once a week is a better compromise than not writing at all. Whichever schedule works best for you, I encourage you to stick with it.

If you write in the same place every day for thirty days in a row, or thirty weeks in a row, you'll form a habit that will be hard to break. And while it may be difficult in the beginning, draw on your reserves of self-discipline and make yourself do it. The rewards will be great.

WHAT SHOULD I INCLUDE IN MY JOURNAL?

Over the course of a day, like a character in a book, you interact with a variety of people in different places, while participating in diverse activities. When you sit down to relate what you did on a given day, you need not recount everything. If you did, you'd have to write pages and pages, and you'd have a volume the size of *War and Peace* by the end of the first month. Instead, I suggest you choose one or two events that stand out in your mind.

An exercise that works well for most people is to sit in a comfortable position in your writing space, close your eyes, and take a deep breath. Think back to when you awakened and replay your day in your mind like a videotape.

Out of everything that happened, pick out the one or two events that captured your attention more than the others. Picture them as vividly as you can. Those are the ones you should write about. On some days, the choices are obvious: birthdays, anniversaries, graduations, births, or the loss of someone we love. These events are milestones in our lives and we should write about them because they affect us so deeply.

For example, some of us have difficulty dealing with another birthday, but it is a once-a-year experience that deserves mention. Perhaps someone gave you a special present. Maybe a friend you hadn't thought about in a very long time sent you a funny card. Perhaps a good friend forgot the date entirely. Whatever the case, record these events so that in the future you can remember them as easily as if you were looking at a photograph.

These occasions, however, occur too infrequently to be the bread and butter subject matter of your journal. For a fuller, more complete look at your life, you must look at the things that happen every day of the year. In other words, look for the unusual cloaked within the usual.

The trick is to keep a ready mind, always looking for that special thing. Perhaps someone performed an act of kindness at the post office, or someone at the grocery store with two overflowing carts let you in line ahead of them since you only had a gallon of milk. Maybe a co-worker who has never said a kind word gave you a well-deserved pat on the back and said, "Good job."

Not only do the real events of our lives provide fodder for our journals, but those nightly visitors called dreams can add dimension to our words. Whether we realize it of not, we all dream. Sometimes our dreams are obscure visions. Sometimes, they are as clear and bright as a Technicolor movie, so touching we feel compelled to tell others. This is the type of dream you may want to include in your journal. Tell why it was so important. Describe its emotional impact, and let someone else peek into a deeper part of your psyche for just a moment.

Write about everything as if you were talking to a dear friend. Tap into that place deep inside yourself and relate your impressions based on senses and emotions. Make the reader see the event through your eyes. Make the reader feel it through your heart, a technique we'll discuss in a later chapter.

Children are also a great source for journal entries, especially when very young. If you've spent any time with young children, I'm sure you've noticed that their perception of the world is not quite like our own. With their limited life experience, they see and hear things a bit differently than we do. They also tend to make the most unexpected connections. Let me give you an example.

One night, shortly after we purchased our first personal computer, we were talking about it over dinner. The conversation revolved around the uses of this marvelous new machine and how our girls, nine and seven at the time, would be able to improve their reports for school as well as play games. Somehow, talk turned to the subject of Guardian Angels and how they fit into our lives.

Our oldest daughter, Regina, said, "I guess they must carry a big notebook around with them all the time to keep track of the good things and bad things we do."

Younger daughter, Julie, adamantly shook her head and said, "You've got to be kidding! Everything's on computer these days!"

Julie's remark has since become part of family lore and it will live on for generations through a journal entry. So when you think about what to include in your diary on any particular day, think about the gift of kindness, the pleasure you derived from someone's humor, or the never-to-be-repeated remark of a child. Those rare moments are to be savored, recorded, and saved for all time.

CHAPTER 4: ABSTRACTS

Ever since mankind developed spoken language, people have gathered to relate and hear of the day's events. Ancient clans revered their storytellers for their knowledge and ability to bring stories of the gods to life, or recount acts of heroism. Today, despite our technology and sophistication, we are not as far removed from those early ancestors as we think. We still gather around a television set or movie screen to watch a good story unfold.

Small children, especially, love to have others read to them, to hear tales from the past, or legends of knights and princesses. They love to listen to the same stories over and over.

Many adults find that curling up in front of a cozy fire with a good book very attractive. Some books capture our imaginations immediately. We become so absorbed in the story that we are compelled to turn the pages to see what happens next. So intent are we on the story that an outside observer might think we were looking for clues to a gold mine. And in a sense we are. We are looking for the wealth of pleasure and knowledge that books give us.

Admittedly, not all books are created equal; some are better than others. Through the years I have come to the conclusion that good writing is good writing, whether it is a romance, a science fiction novel, a mystery, or a journal. The bottom line is that whether a novel or a journal, good writing does not just happen. You must craft your diary so that future generations who read it will gain not only understanding and insight, but enjoyment, too.

Having read hundreds of books, I believe that all good novels share two important elements: a great plot and wonderful characterization. Perhaps that's an oversimplification, but anything else you consider about a novel will fall into one of those two categories. Authors of fiction use certain techniques to tell their story and make readers care about the characters they create. These fiction techniques are important in your journal writing as well.

Compelling plot or subject matter is important to a book because without it, there's nothing to keep the reader interested enough to turn the pages. I love to read during lunch and just before I retire for the night. Often I'll determine a stopping point long before I reach it, such as the end of a chapter. Too often, once I arrive at my destination, I just can't close the book because I want to know what happens next. That's a compelling plot.

Well-defined, well-developed characters are also a necessary element of a good book. A good writer will show who the character is and what's going on inside his or her head instead of telling the reader. In this way the reader experiences the story through the senses and emotions of the characters. What did they see? What did they feel? Without that involvement, readers will simply put the book down and may never pick it up again.

If a book is missing either of these elements or treats them poorly, we tend to view the story as incomplete or unsatisfying. Making these elements part of your journal writing technique will improve your writing in more ways than you ever dreamed possible.

PLOT

If someone were to ask you about the plot of the last book you read, your response would include what happened in the story. The plot is no more than the sequence of events and how they unfold. Your journal is no different, except that the plot develops on a day-to-day basis. Instead of constructing a plot for an entire book, your job is to plot and write about each scene you choose from your day.

During your journal writing time, as you determine what events to include for that particular day, think about what happened and how it happened. Ask yourself about the places you went, the people you saw, the things you did. Below are some suggested questions to jog your memory:

Where were you?

What were you doing there?

Whom were you with?

What were they like?

Whom did you meet?

What did you do?

What did you accomplish?

What will you do as the result of this?

What time of day was it?

To help you remember all the important points of an event, replay in your head much as you would a videotape from beginning to end—in living color. See the place and the people. Review any conversations you had. Once you are sure of the sequence of events, think about the details.

Since we can only perceive things through our senses, it is important to call upon all five of them—taste, sight, smell, hearing, touch—and incorporate them in our writing. Such inclusion is called sensory description. Most people tend to rely most heavily on sight and sound, and in your early efforts you will too, but don't discount the other senses. They are very powerful and we rely upon them more than we realize. To help with your sensory descriptions, ask yourself questions like:

What did it taste like?

What did it look like?

What did it smell like?

What did it sound like?

What did it feel like?

It's not necessary to tap into all five senses for every entry, but certainly, if you can employ two or three, your writing will be much richer for it.

Remember, this is your way to reach out to the future and share an experience with someone you'll never meet. You want him or her to experience things not only through your eyes, but through every other fiber of your being. That introduces emotion, another aspect you should include in your writing.

I've attended several art fairs that displayed a variety of paintings done in pastels, oils, and acrylics. Most of the work I've seen is very good, yet it always seems one work of art will stand out from the rest. It took me a while to discover the difference between the art I thought was good and art that truly touched me.

Often, I encounter a painting that is mechanically correct—that is, the artist has a grasp of light and shadows, shape and line. Perspective is perfect and the colors are clear. Yet, I can walk by without a second look.

A few feet further on, I notice another painting done in the same medium. As I approach, I anticipate stopping to study it. When I'm near enough to look more closely, I may be able to tell immediately that something is not quite right—perhaps the perspective is slightly off. Yet, it touches me and I want to reach out and touch it in return, maybe even take it home.

The difference between the two is the emotion the artist was able to convey through the brush, to the canvas, and in turn to me.

Similarly, computers can be programmed to write a story or paint a picture. But neither is art if it is devoid of emotion, and neither will touch the person who sees it or reads it.

When you write in your journal, it is important not only to tap into your five senses, but your emotions as well. This is the time for you to let what you feel flow onto the page. No one is standing over your shoulder to chide you for your sentimentality or scold you if you confess to feeling anger. Whatever you feel, be honest with yourself and your reader: write it down.

Let me demonstrate how important it is to take a little time to tap into your emotions, as well as your senses, when you write your journal entries. First, take a look at the following entry.

It snowed last night.

These are simply four words strung together to make a grammatically correct, matter-of-fact statement conveying little more than a weather report for a given time. A hundred years from now someone will read that sentence and think little or nothing about it But, with a little creativity and emotion, you can make those four words into something magical.

With my hand against the glass, I stood at the kitchen window and watched the white flakes drift softly to earth like so many feathers. The night sky looked like a velvet curtain, a backdrop for the glittering diamonds that reflected the brightness of street lights. Life outside stood still and silent for a few brief hours as everyone sheltered from the storm, but I brought my cold fingers to the smile on my face and thought of the fun I'd have playing in the icy white mounds tomorrow.

For some of you, the previous paragraph may seem too romantic a look at a snowstorm. Instead, you might prefer your journal entry to take a more pragmatic tone. That's fine. You can be very practical and still make use of sensory description.

The windshield wipers beat a steady rhythm to the country western song playing on my car radio. I waited at the red light and marveled at how slowly the traffic moved as the snow accumulated on the streets. The temperature seemed to drop by the minute as everyone's temper seemed to rise. The light flashed green and my own frustration grew as I tried to pull out into the intersection only to hear my tires slip and slide across the ice. But that frustration quickly turned to icy fear as the back of my car fishtailed and I spun a hundred and eighty degrees in the middle of the road.

Both paragraphs describe the same snowstorm, but each is from a very different point of view, by people with very different personalities. But they both describe the scene using the senses and emotions. One of the most entertaining things about journal writing is finding your own style, a style that not only fits your personality, but a style that will tell the reader about you.

Practice writing with a few paragraphs of your own. Start with something easy. Pick a topic and include two senses. Pick another and write only about the emotion. Choose a third and include three senses and emotion. Practice. Have fun with it, and you'll surprise yourself at how well you can write. While you should feel free to choose any topic you like, below are a few suggestions to help you get started:

Meeting your best friend for the first time

Bringing home your first new car

Introducing your date to your parents

Your thoughts when you saw a newborn baby

How you fell in love

Your first time away from home

A traumatic birthday

The loss of someone you love

After you've had some time to familiarize yourself with putting sensory description together with emotion in a paragraph, perfect the technique in your own journal. It will soon become automatic.

In my workshops, I always ask if anyone in the group would like to read his or her paragraph aloud. Usually one or two brave souls volunteer to share what they have written. I'm always amazed at how much talent people harbor within them. The quality of the writing always earns the applause and admiration of the rest of the group. All it takes is a little instruction and practice.

CHARACTERS

While sensory description and emotion play a big part in your writing, so do the characters, the people who move through your life. Friends, relatives, acquaintances, and co-workers each play distinct roles. They, like us, are unique individuals with characteristics all their own.

When you write about them in your journal, you should describe them the first time you mention them. Physical characteristics such as height, weight, color of hair and eyes are the easiest, and they help give future readers a clear picture of the person you're writing about.

The real challenge comes when you try to describe the essence of that person's personality, another aspect of characterization. This is more difficult to write about than physical characteristics, because you must show the reader through descriptions of a person's behavior. In other words, if someone you know is selfish, don't simply say that person is selfish—show his or her selfishness by giving an example of that person's behavior.

The following sentences show exactly what I mean:

My sister Nancy is a selfish pig!

I can understand a child writing that sentence in anger. But while it may be effective in conveying emotion, we don't know why the writer feels this way. On the other hand, if we expand on it just a bit, to describe Nancy's actions, the reader can draw their own conclusions about Nancy.

> *There was only one piece of mother's wonderful almond fudge left in the dish. Without asking any of the rest of us if we wanted a share, Nancy scooped it up and popped it into her mouth.*

BRINGING IT ALL TOGETHER

Now that we have discussed the elements of a good book, let's bring them together into a single paragraph. As an example, we'll use a simple, grammatically correct statement.

Stephen started kindergarten today.

So what? Boring! The entry fails to stand out in any way. Hundreds of thousands of other children across the country started kindergarten on that same day. The entry is devoid of sensory description and emotion. It tells nothing of what happened before the boy left for school or what his mother or father felt. Now, if you tap into the emotion of the event and the senses, the entry might look something like the following paragraphs:

This morning as Stephen ate his oatmeal at the kitchen table, he could hardly contain his excitement. I could barely control my tears as I straightened the collar of his new blue shirt. Today was his first day of kindergarten. I made sure his denim book bag was properly packed, and as I counted the pencils and crayons one last time, I mentally calculated all the times I had walked the floor with him when he was sick or comforted him when he fell and skinned his knee.

Hand in hand we walked to the end of the driveway to wait for the big yellow bus that would take him to school. He was all smiles and so excited that he jumped up and down as the bus came down the street. He ran on board and found a seat, then he turned and waved as it drove him away. I waved back and brushed a tear from my cheek.

Much more interesting than simply stating, "Stephen started kindergarten today." From the above paragraph, the reader knows many things about Stephen and his parent. Yes, Stephen started kindergarten, but we also know what the writer did and what the writer saw and felt. We know that this parent and child are close, that this little boy is active and happy, and that this parent is a bit sentimental. Imagine if you had an entire journal comprising such entries! Most of us don't have such a treasure from the past, but you have the opportunity to create one for the future.

CHAPTER 5: ADDITIONAL INSIGHTS

With a little practice and some patience, your writing technique will improve very quickly, especially if you write every day. But no matter how well you learn to set your words on paper, there may be something else you'd like to include in your diary to make it more complete—pictures. No matter how wonderful a description you read of the Santa Elena Canyon on the Rio Grande, you cannot truly appreciate its rugged beauty until you see it. The same holds true for people.

As I research my family history and find bits and pieces of information, I have yet to come across a picture of an ancestor taken before 1900. I wish I knew what my great-grandparents looked like. I wish I had a picture of their family and home, and then I put myself in the place of my descendants as they read my journal. They'll want to know what I and others looked like. They'll be curious about the way we dressed, the furniture we used, the cars we drove. So don't feel shy. Include photographs of all kinds in your journal. When you go on vacation, buy postcards expressly for your journal.

If anything about you appeared in the local newspaper, or you received an award, include at least a copy in your journal. Perhaps you saw something in the newspaper that made you laugh. Cut it out and include that in your journal as well. I know a woman who likes to include comics from her morning newspaper that she finds especially funny and then tell why it made her chuckle.

To make your journal more interesting, you could also include musings about what you think the future will bring. Have a little fun and try to predict what transportation, politics, or medicine will be like in a hundred years. What do you think education or fashion will be like? Give your imagination free rein, and a complete picture of you, including the physical, emotional, and intellectual facets of your personality, will emerge. Those who know us now take these aspects for granted, but they are the things that people in the future will want to know about us.

Whatever you add to your journal, be aware of available preservation techniques to ensure that you will harm neither your journal nor the photos or other pieces of memorabilia you include. There are several good preservation books on the market, such as *A Preservation Guide: Saving the Past and the Present for the Future,* by Barbara Sagraves (Ancestry, 1995). Make the extra effort to take care of your journal and its contents. Remember, this is the part of you that will travel through time.

Part 3
The Rewards

CHAPTER 6: FINDING THE JOY

In previous chapters we have discussed the how and why of creative journals. Each day or week, as you record the events of your life, you must keep in mind that you are creating a wonderful legacy for future generations. But what do you get out of all this?

Thus far, we've covered only some of the benefits of keeping a journal: the quiet time for reflection it allows, the time to consider your value, the realization of the worth of the things you do, and the personal growth it brings. In fact, I know some people who include these reflections in their entries to bring their daily entry to a conclusion. There are, however, even greater benefits.

More and more, scientific research confirms what medical professionals and patients have thought for a very long time: that the mind and body are intricately intertwined. The mind (that piece of ourselves that stands apart from our physical body—our soul, our psyche, that place where hopes and dreams reside—can affect the physical body.

A positive attitude helps patients to cope, to boost their immune systems, and sometimes even to heal their diseases. No one can explain it, but there is more to us than our physical selves. Doctors encourage their patients to keep journals, and the results are remarkable. Every one of us can reap tremendous benefits by tapping into the enormous power to heal both the physical and emotional hurts in our lives.

In the annotated bibliography at the end of this book, I have listed several magazine articles that address specific physical and emotional benefits of keeping a journal. If your local library doesn't have them, it can get copies for you in a few days through interlibrary loan.

Last of all, your journal will be a constant reminder that your life is not boring and that someday, someone is going to want to read about you. I'd wager that my great-grandparents thought their lives tremendously boring, getting up before dawn to draw water from the well, but I wish they had written about it.

You probably don't draw water from a well, but you do many other things that will be uncommon one hundred years from now. That reason alone is enough to make your actions worthwhile. Take time at the end of each day or week to think about all the things you've done, all the places you've been, all the people you've met. Perhaps you smiled at someone who was having a particularly bad day. That may become your journal entry because of how you felt when you saw their eyes light up and you realized you had made someone feel better.

Maybe there was a specific business deal that you worked very hard to complete. With persistence, you overcame all the obstacles and triumphed. Or you may have encountered a child who fell and skinned his or her knee. With tears streaming, the child came running to you for comfort. With a snug hug and a bandage, you kissed the tears away.

Perhaps you were in the middle of a crisis and someone full of compassion and empathy came to your aid. Their caring made you realize you were not alone and that you were someone worth helping. Sometimes the smallest human touch is all we need to remind us of the Divine within us.

I could list example after example, but this is intended to be a small book. Now that you know what to look for, take the time to find situations like this in your daily life. They are there every day. All you need do is keep your heart and your mind open to them.

And when you realize that you and what you do play such a wonderful part of others' lives, you will in turn experience a feeling of fulfillment. You will realize

CHAPTER 6: JUST DO IT

*N*ow that you understand the importance of keeping a creative journal, it's time to sit down and do it. Begin with the mechanics and determine how you will record your words and thoughts. Go to the stationery store and pick out a special pen to write with. Weigh it in your hands to see how it feels. Wrap your fingers around it in a caress and ready yourself to put down your thoughts for posterity.

Set a definite time and place to be alone to write in your journal. Sift through the day's events and choose the one that had the most impact on you, then write it down with as much detail as you can remember. Incorporate your senses and emotions so that readers to come will feel it as you did.

Remember the elements you enjoy in a good book and include them in your writing. The characters are the people we come into contact with, and the plot is the never-ending series of events in life. Allow yourself the luxury of pouring your heart out onto the page.

Incorporate all of these things into your writing. Write a journal that others will want to read and one that may indeed be the basis for a terrific book one day. Keep in mind the great-grandchild or the stranger who someday in the future will wish they had known you. Keeping a journal today is like stepping into the future and handing it to them with the words, "Here I am."

We can hope that as they take our book into their hands, they will take our words into their hearts.

APPENDIX: TIPS TO MAKE YOUR WRITING GREAT!

As a professional writer, I guarantee that what you write will almost never come out right the first time. Have patience, and give yourself credit for what you do write; then put your work away until the next day for editing, just before you begin to write your new entry. You'll be able to view what you have written more objectively and do a much better job of editing.

You'll also notice that from day to day as you write in your journal and internalize some of the tips for good writing, you'll find yourself making fewer mistakes and developing a good, strong writing style. Here are some tips for good writing and things to look for when you edit yourself.

I. ACTIVE VOICE

One of the quickest ways for a writer to put a reader to sleep is to write in the passive voice. Passive voice does exactly what its name implies: it makes the action passive. I remember vividly to this day the example my fourth grade teacher gave as the difference between active voice and passive voice.

She picked up an eraser and flung it across the room. Those of us sitting beneath the flight path ducked and fortunately escaped the flying eraser.

She pointed to the back corner and said, "The eraser was thrown across the room. Passive voice! We don't know who threw it, just that it happened."

She repeated the action. This time we didn't bother to duck since we realized her aim was good enough. She pointed again and said, *"I threw the eraser across the room. Active voice! We know who did it and what they did."*

A sentence in the active voice states specifically who performed the action. Look at what you have written and circle the verbs that are some form of the verb "to be" such as *am, is, are, was, were, been.* Also look for auxiliary or helping verbs such as *have, had,* and *has.* See if you can substitute active, past tense verbs that end in "t," "d," or "ed" for these passive verbs. They will make your writing stronger and more interesting.

Example: The store window was broken by a car and the glass was found on the sidewalk.

Revised: The car careened through the store window, and the glass shattered over the sidewalk.

2. "ING" VERBS
Look at what you have written and circle verbs that end in "ing." Think of a way to make them simple past tense verbs that end in "t," "d," or "ed."

Example: Standing by the stove, Claire was stirring the pot of stew.

Revised: Claire stood by the stove and stirred the pot of stew.

3. STRINGS
Another problem to watch for is long strings of adjectives and adverbs. You may have a lot to say about size, shape, color, and other characteristics, but don't jam all your descriptive words together in one sentence. Sometimes two or three sentences work better.

Example: She cried when she saw her long, blue, velvet, Paris-designed gown dragging in the dust of the Texas street behind her.

Revised: The blue gown dragged along the street. Her heart broke when she saw the train of the velvet dress, its Paris folds full of Texas dust. That was the last straw. She crumpled to the ground and cried.

4. UNNECESSARY WORDS

Get rid of words you don't need. Try to say what you have to say in the most efficient way possible and still be descriptive and emotional.

Example: Mary looked up into the night sky at the twinkling stars and made a wish.

Revised: Mary looked into the night sky and wished upon a star.

5. SHOW DON'T TELL

When you express feelings in your writing, demonstrate such emotion through behavior: don't tell me someone was angry, show me.

Example: Clint left the room in anger.

Revised: Clint stomped from the room and slammed the door behind him.

6. LONG SENTENCES

Avoid sentences that are too long. There is no rule that says a good sentence must contain twenty words. If anything, shorter, more efficient sentences are the mark of crisp writing. Break the information in one extra long sentence into two or three sentences. Or, perhaps, use independent clauses with semi-colons. Varying sentence length also adds variety to your writing and keeps a reader interested.

Example: Miriam could never help herself when she went shopping and hit a sale because she always thought it was a great way to save money and get something she needed anyway.

Revised: Miriam loved to shop during sales. She figured it was a great way to get what she needed and save money besides. Her only problem was that she didn't know when to stop.

7. OVERUSED WORDS

Try not to use the same word over and over. Sometimes it's unavoidable, but often, you can eliminate some of the repetitions completely or use other words to express the same thought using words called "synonyms." A thesaurus is a helpful tool for this purpose and will help you expand your working vocabulary at the same time. If you use a computer, your word processing software may include a thesaurus.

Example: Mary knew the journey would take six weeks. It was a journey she had been looking forward to for a long, long time. She knew the perils that awaited her on this journey, but was ready to face each one of them time and time again.

Revised: Mary had been looking forward to this voyage for many years. She knew the journey would present her with many obstacles, but undaunted by the perils, steeled herself to meet each one in its turn.

LAST WORDS

Now that you know the basic techniques that can make your writing interesting, write as you have never written before. You will fill the hearts of your readers for many years to come.

A further testament to the growing interest in journals is the proliferation of articles in popular magazines about journal keeping. The articles target everyone from young people to senior citizens, from runners to arthritics. Below is a small sampling of articles that have appeared in recent years that discuss journaling in a variety of ways. You can find copies of these and many other articles at your local library.

There are also some excellent published journals of well-known people available at your favorite bookstore or local library. Search for them in your library's card catalogue or ask your research librarian for help in locating them. Both the articles and the published journals make for interesting reading and I'm sure you will take away some valuable ideas for your own diary.

Aaron, Daniel. "The Great Diarist" (George Templeton Strong, American Diarist), *American Heritage,* March 1988. Discusses the diary of George Templeton Strong with a strong historical and political perspective.

Abercrombie, Barbara. "Keeping a Journal," *The Writer,* March 1991. For anyone who wishes to write anything, this is an excellent article offering encouragement and suggestions to develop the discipline to write every day.

Bell, Alison. "Journal Writing: Staying in Touch with Yourself," *Teen Magazine,* October 1991. Targets teenage girls and discusses the benefits of keeping a personal journal.

Benn, Tony. "Writing Your Own History," *History Today*, April 1987. Discusses diaries from a political point of view.

Berendt, John. "The Diary: What Matters Most, Who Reads It," *Esquire*, March 1994. Discusses the discipline required to make journal entries every day and how most writers fail to reread what they have written.

Brown, Gayle. "The Healing Power of the Journal: Easing the Ups and Downs of Arthritis," *Arthritis Today*, January-February 1993. This article deals with the daily challenges faced by those who suffer chronic arthritis and suggests using a journal to help cope and improve their quality of life.

Bultman, Judith. "Diaries for My Children," *Parents Magazine*, March, 1991. Bultman has written an interesting article about a mother's diaries and the promise that they will one day provide her children with insight into themselves and their family.

Cunningham, Amy. "Private Papers: The Story of Your Life Starts with a Well-Kept Journal," *Mademoiselle*, July 1991. Another article that encourages young people to keep a journal as a learning tool.

Eller, Daryn. "The Dieter's Secret Weapon," *Mademoiselle*, March 1992. Shows dieting readers how to use a journal to make behavioral changes.

Henderson, Joe. "Stride by Scribe: Consider Turning Your Training Log into a Diary," *Runner's World*, May 1993. Physical fitness is important to many for whom running is part of their daily regimen. This article offers suggestions for using a daily log to help improve training and fitness.

Hoagland, Edward. "A Writer's Journal," *Harper's Magazine*, February 1989. Gives insights into the mind of a writer who keeps a journal.

Latvala, Charlotte. "The Joy of Keeping a Diary," *Cosmopolitan,* May 1993. Latvala discusses her own love affair with journal writing and how to make use of one's diary as a therapist and confidant in good times and bad.

Nicola, Karen. "Pain on Paper: Keeping a Grief Recovery Journal," *Vibrant Life,* November-December 1992. After the death of her young son, Nicola learned to work through her grief and pain through the pages of her diary.

Raphael, Maryanne. "Should You Keep A Diary?" *The Writer,* January 1987. This is an interesting article discussing the pros and cons of keeping a diary. If you have any doubts about whether or not you should keep a journal, this article will persuade you to buy a manuscript book and a pen and start writing immediately.

ABOUT THE AUTHOR

*J*oan R. Neubauer established herself as a freelance writer in 1987 and has since sold a variety of articles to both regional and national publications. A graduate of West Chester University in Pennsylvania, Joan taught Spanish and English as a Second Language for a number of years before pursuing a second career as a writer.

In 1990, she founded Word Wright International as a copywriting firm to serve the writing needs of Houston's business community. However, Joan soon recognized a different need, and her company now specializes in helping people write their life stories.

On the subject of autobiographies, Joan says: "They are by far the most enthralling adventures I've had as a writer, and they make me wonder how many other wonderful stories there are to tell."

In addition to writing, she teaches classes, conducts workshops, and frequently addresses groups where she educates her audiences as a businesswoman, educator, and writer.

NOTES

NOTES

NOTES

NOTES

NOTES